Victorious
Words to Survive by.

Daily inspired words for everyone from everywhere.
The 'Om' of Yoga.
For years, I have collected words others say to themselves, words to survive on that bring joy, hope, distraction, and inspiration from yoga teachers, students, poets, and the Akashic records. May these words help all others get through life a little easier and less alone.

Troy Cox

Safe Yoga School Publications

Copyright 2024 Troy Cox

All rights reserved, including the right to reproduce this book or portions thereof in any form whatsoever. For information about special discounts for bulk purchases please contact via email trainertroy@gmail.com

Published by Safe Yoga School, LLC

These are a collection of words from a variety of sources handed down second hand. I honor any request to remove portions of the selection if they infringe on any rights.

All artwork within is original and created by Troy Cox

@Trainer Troy Yoga on social media.

Troy Cox

www.trainertroy.com

ISBN:9781727027778

Publisher and Distributor: Safe Yoga School Publications

Owner of Safe Yoga School and yoga teacher since 2002, has traveled and taught in India, Bali, Costa Rica and across the U.S from Los Angeles to Orlando.

Author of the 'Why of Yoga' four years of interviews of why everyone is doing yoga. Troy Cox

Private Stretching, Yoga, Meditation lessons, Teacher Training, Eating Coaching and Life Management Coach

500 Hour ERYT Yoga Alliance Yoga Facilitator

Corporate Services Available

(407) 285 8719

www.safeyogaschool.com

My YouTube channel: @TrainerTroyYoga

Amazon Authors Page Troy Cox

In class, I often ask my students to close their eyes and think of a word, thought, prayer, poem, or mantra that brings them joy. I encourage them to allow the words to create a feeling and notice as they spread through the body. Words are indeed powerful, and their energy and imagery can work to lift us up. I began to ask my students what words they were speaking to themselves. This is a collection of their words of hope and joy, and some I added of my own. My hope is these words bring light and love to all who read and share them.
-Troy Cox

Victorious 'Words to Survive by.'

Read in the morning, at night or for shavasana pose in yoga.

"Give everyone an equal chance, but if they can't laugh, forget about it."

-Ed Cox

VICTORIOUS
Words to Survive by.

Words of Joy, Hope, and Inspiration: A Collection from Yoga Teachers, Students, Poets, and Beyond

Dive into a curated collection of uplifting and transformative words lovingly gathered from the hearts of yoga teachers, devoted students, celebrated poets, and voices of wisdom from all walks of life. This inspiring collection offers mantras, affirmations, and quotes that light the way through life's challenges, providing comfort, strength, and boundless hope. Let these words be your beacon, guiding you to inner peace, resilience, and a renewed sense of purpose. Embrace the power of positivity and let it illuminate your path.

Troy Cox
Trainer Troy

Words that others use to survive by, inspire and repeat every day. Poems, prayers, mantras, and inspirations. To be read at shavasana, nighttime or anytime.

1st edition

This book is dedicated to all those who are inspired from thoughts, words, actions, and deeds. The words of teachers, family, friends, saints and loved ones that uplift and carry us forward.
Words to survive by.
-Troy Cox

CONTENTS

Introduction	2
Dedication	10
Book Statement	14
Acknowledgements	16
Bio	19
Forward	21
Chapter One Purification, Water	26
Chapter Two Possibilities, Earth	48
Chapter Three Protection, Fire	63
Your Victorious words, a Reflection Journal	73

I have collected the voices of students, teachers, mentors and loved ones. I have asked them what words bring them joy and happiness and they have shared. Poems, prayers, mantras, song lyrics or any words that bring a sense of peace and calm. We all have them and say them to ourselves to keep us going. I have collected a few here and hope they help others as much as they have inspired me.

In class I often ask my students to close their eyes and think of a word, thoughts, prayer, poem, or mantra that brings them joy. I encourage them to allow the words to create a feeling and notice as they spread through the body. Words are indeed powerful, and their energy and imagery can work to lift us up. I began to ask my students what words they were speaking to themselves. These are a collection of their words of hope and joy and some that I added of my own. My hope is these words bring light and love to all those who read them and that they are shared.

– Namaste, Troy Cox

"I have found that in any difficult situation, when I make the choice to do what is best for me, and honor my soul, that it ultimately is the best decision for everyone involved."

-Kristi Vanato

What words do you or your family say to themselves to get through the toughest days?

This is the question I asked many students after class in my research for this book. Take a moment to write down your own here.

Words to Om by. Daily inspired words from everywhere.

Words to Om by. Daily inspired words from everywhere.

INTRODUCTION

One word, spoken with intention, can inspire great change in a person, nation, or the whole universe.

August 2009 Scotland. I suffered a terrible bicycle wreck. Hitting the wrong brake, I flipped over the handlebars, landed on my face, and wound up with a mouth full of broken teeth, split lips, and shredded skin. The helmet saved my life. Lying in a pool of blood, facing downhill, not sure how bad I was hurt, feeling panic overcoming me, beginning to hyperventilate, I knew if I did, I might die from asphyxiation. One of the biking group leaned over me, she seemed to appear out of air and whispered to me to take a breath and try to relax. She placed her hand on my center back. As soon as she touched me, I was instantly calm, and my yoga teacher appeared in my mind, floating in lotus position, smiling, projecting a light of protection. I knew her words took me out of panic, and I stayed calm for the entire rest of the E.R. visit and ride home in the taxi in the early morning hours. Her words, so sweetly spoken in my ear, 'Try to take a breath and relax, help is on the way,' resonated in my head for days after, as did the E.R. doctors. He told me a teenage boy had died the day before from the same type of accident and only my helmet saved my life.

Words inspire, uplift, help others, and bring inspiration. They are spoken by teachers, lovers, the lost, and leaders. Life and its many journeys can be challenging and traumatizing.

Words to Om by. Daily inspired words from everywhere.

I wanted to use the words of my teachers and students to inspire. When I ask people who are lying down at the end of yoga to think of words that bring them joy, I am touched by the smiles that usually grow on their faces. These words help them, uplift them, are memorized, and are part of their consciousness. Language has evolved over centuries as a means of communicating feelings, emotions, thoughts, and deeds. Their messages can cross cultures, religions, races, and all boundaries that divide.

Allow these words to travel within your experience. To permeate your consciousness, to marinate all day. See how they are filtered by your own unique experience and how you react to them. Observe as the words on the page make their way into your day through your contemplation of them. Then, when they have been thought on for a day, move on to the next.

Some words will become part of your life, and others will float in and out. The ones that matter to you will stick; the others are for another time. Let them go. Keep the words that bring you the feeling of victory over the situation. Use them as a tool to help you or help others with them.

Thank you for the opportunity to share what I have been given.
May you be filled with love and light,
Namaste.

Words to Om by. Daily inspired words from everywhere.

What is communication?

The last pose in yoga class is Shavasana, The Corpse Pose. Its ultimate message is the deep integration of the entire mental and physical experience that yoga can lead to. Once that deep feeling of the experience happens, an awakening can occur. If guided into a deep state of relaxation, either on the mat in meditation or a flowing posture-based practice, a union can happen. A person could potentially feel a deep connection with themselves, usually reserved for a private experience and realize there is a different perspective to every situation. Many sources can lead to the same light. Amrit Desai inspired me to my core when, during one talk at the institute, he said to us that we are all like the sun. We come from the same source, but each ray is uniquely expressed. We are like one sun, many rays. My wish is that this book will bring peace, calm, and focus to many from the same source but expressed in a unique way.

This book is the sum of experiencing words coming through me in Shavasana posture as I guided a class into their last pose. I could feel the words coming through me as I spoke, but I noticed I had not thought of the words. As I heard the words spoken aloud in my voice, I did not know what I was about to say. I realized that my decision making had been removed and as I thought it I spoke it.

Words to Om by. Daily inspired words from everywhere.

After class, students would ask me to repeat what I had said in Shavasana. I could not recall. I did not remember thinking about what I would say, only hearing it as I said it out loud. I knew the words had been inspired by the feeling in the room in that moment. After I guide students into resting position, laying on the back, arms at the side, palms up, and neck in neutral. Then, I speak what I consider guidance into relaxation, followed by silence. So, during the silent whisper of students breathing, I began to try and jot down what I had said on a pad. Partly for my own records but also to reflect on myself. That was the genesis of this book. As I usually do I ask others about their experiences to find a common thread. Whenever I had a conversation like this with someone and something they said or mentioned struck a chord in me, I would tell them about this book. I wanted to know more about what kept them going in life, and I wanted to share it.

Life tends to change like the seasons. One day, it is summer, and the next it has turned into winter. What do we say to ourselves on this adventure called life to keep us going through the harder times? What things do we say to ourselves in the Spring and Summer times of our lives to keep us motivated and happy? We, as humans, are diverse and varied in many ways. We are also the same in other ways. In yogic studies, the threads that tie objects together are called 'sutras.' My life adventure happened when I was only seven years old. My father got the orders that we were being sent to Japan. The awe-inspiring sights, cultural history, and religious practices have stayed with me my entire life. I will never forget the trips to Mt. Fujisan, the temples with enormous gongs, and the exotic flavors and deserts. That experience truly showed a little boy how grand and diverse life can be. How different and unique yet similar we all really are. I always try my best to find what connects us to others.

Words to Om by. Daily inspired words from everywhere.

Yoga just showed me a vehicle to express that desire to see how we are so similar yet having vastly different life experiences. What is it these fellow travelers say to themselves when they are alone, inspired, uninspired, flying high, or sinking low? This is my field research on the subject. Some of the words are mine, some are quotes others have shared, and some are from those who have been my teachers in life. My wish in compiling these words that have brought myself and others solace is that the words will live on. They will take a life of their own and live to inspire others.

World renowned Yoga Nidra pioneer Shri Shri Kamini Desai wrote the following on communication:

"There are four ways, and only four ways, in which we have contact with the world. We are evaluated and classified by these four contacts: what we do, how we look, what we say, and how we say it."-Kamini Desai

Taking vocal training, public speaking, projection for the actor, diction, and voice-over classes for many years has enhanced my ability to use my voice as an effective means of communication. I can easily modulate my tonality and volume to affect a mood or meaning in my directions as a teacher. What if, just by your voice, you could make someone 'feel' what you were trying to relay? This is the basis of Sanskrit, the ancient language of Yoga. An energy exchange through words.

Words to Om by. Daily inspired words from everywhere.

As actors in theater, we can relay to the audience the mood of our character. Just because the character I am playing is angry, I do not need to go through the stress of getting angry. I can use the volume and diction of my voice and the words of the author to relay the mood of my character.

The tone of voice shows our concern for the audience and determines in the minds of the audience whether we are sincere. The audience may say a speaker is boring even though the content is very stimulating. It's the monotone voice that makes them think the presentation is dull. The words that the author chose are specific. In most theatre productions, the author does not like their words to be changed. They labored hours in writing and editing to precisely use words that will affect the mood and emotion of their story. The actor's job is then to choose the way those words will be delivered. The meaning the actor puts behind his words comes from what they are feeling while they deliver their words.

According to the Linguistic Society of America, there may be more than 6,909 languages and families of languages spoken in the world. 'Very different languages can share words while different speakers of the "same" language may vary widely in their vocabulary due to factors of education or speaking style. Different languages may display the same sentence patterns, while a single language may display a great variety of patterns.' Stephen R. Anderson: *How many languages are there in the world?*

Words to Om by. Daily inspired words from everywhere.

There are so many ways to communicate from one person to another. Languages, written words, singing, dance and art are forms of getting a message from one place to the next. Proper communication is vital to our survival. Miscommunication can lead to frustration, emotional responses and has even led to war. The only real way to connect with another living being is by communicating from the heart. It takes bravery and trust to open your heart while sharing your thoughts on the world. We respect our artists because they dare to express universal ideas that most of us would be unable to express. Poets, authors, singers, dancers, and orators can translate views on life in a way that seems revolutionary. They capture our imagination and allow us to see things in a different world. They can only make that connection when they access their hearts, and we open ours to see their message. Opening your heart can mean many things, we can try to do it alone, but it often requires being receptive to accepting love and intimacy from another. Intimate or with friends, family members, teachers, and even strangers, we can find the trust to allow our heart to open. Once the trust in ourselves has been encouraged, we can eventually allow our heart to remain open even in stressful situations that life presents, disagreements with others, and life's challenges. As we work on physical, mental, and emotional tools that help us to stay open, we may even begin to understand empathy.

One time, while listening to my teacher and all the students sharing their transformative experiences, I raised my hand. I told the Guru that I thought I finally understood the meaning of empathy. Everyone laughed, including my teacher, so I smiled and laughed too. But what they did not know was that I was serious. I had always been impatient with most excuses for not doing. Now, while listening to others' life stories I experienced an opening of my heart. I saw others do the same and I could connect to them in a way I never dreamed possible. I felt what they had gone through. We had one heart.
May this collection of words shared with me from open hearts and received with an open heart help to inspire, uplift, and perhaps connect to the heart.

Words to Om by. Daily inspired words from everywhere.

Words to Om by. Daily inspired words from everywhere.

Troy Cox

DEDICATION

This book is dedicated to all of you who question and search for understanding of this human condition. The students, who have also been my teachers, are continually challenging me with questions that I seek out answers as well. Hopefully, this book will help answer some of your personal questions through the sharing of others' paths of discovery. To my mother and father who have consistently reminded me to be all that I can be and give to others through humor while maintaining resolve. My mother taught me strength and to get back up when knocked down, and my father taught me how to laugh again after nine years of not laughing after my brother went before us. Truly, I have been blessed by such loving and kind parents, thank you. Debbie, thank you for always being the unfaltering wind beneath my wings. To my teachers, Molly Knight, my writing would not exist without your example of boldly creating your own voice and bravely putting it out there, Diane Ross, Yogi Amrit Desai, Neem Kiroli Baba, Pramahansa Yogananda, Amma, Swami Kripalu, Jesus Christ, Ram Das, and my first true teacher and Guru, my brother, Todd E. Cox. Todd, you were the best little brother who never complained about my endless taunting, and you have been more of a man than I can ever be, guiding me on the other side. Thank you for leading me to all my teachers and Gurus Todd. I created and named my yoga technique after my brother's initials: Total Engagement Concept; Todd E. Cox. Love you brother.

Words to Om by. Daily inspired words from everywhere.

And these expressions, trials, and tribulations shared within could not be possible without the generous sharing, love, and journey of the many students who have graced me with their presence along my own journey. Through struggle or great ease, I thank you for the lessons. For they are truly not my students, but my teachers. This book is for you.

I give thanks to all my guides, angels, arc angels, loved one and those on my lineage that have gone before me. May the light bearers who have illuminated my path have their light returned to them in multitudes and may I have the strength to carry their light to others. The light in myself recognizes the light in you and the point where we merge as one.

I am thankful for all students who have taken a class, training, or workshop, for you are my teachers I will never forget.

Namaste! Love Troy Cox

Author's note. These words are from others. If any violate copyright laws, please notify me and they will be removed. I own no rights to any of the words held within that I have not written on my own.

Words to Om by. Daily inspired words from everywhere.

BOOKS BY TROY

Y.?.O.G.A.

The 'Om' of Yoga: Victorious. Words to Survive by.
is part of an intended series examining spirituality and yoga.
Look for the other books in the series.

- **'The Why of Yoga'.** 'Y' is everybody doing yoga? Four years of interviews about why the world is doing yoga and why not to do yoga.

Y. The Why of Yoga?
O. The Om of Yoga. Victorious: Words to Survive by.
G. The Life of a Teacher, not a guru.
A. Ascension, the science of enlightenment, is it real?

Words to Om by. Daily inspired words from everywhere.

Words to Om by. Daily inspired words from everywhere.

BOOK STATEMENT

What do others say to themselves to keep them in joy and happiness? The goal or aim of this book is to share a personal account from teachers and students I have met along my path of what words keep them going forward. To share insight into the words that others say to themselves to bring joy, happiness, and light into their own lives.

The hope in these words, which helped others in their challenges and can also inspire hope in others. All around the world, people are facing similar challenges in life but sometimes feel so isolated and alone in their experiences. Through the various personal words, prayers, mantras, and poems, I will try to find a commonality in how others deal with ups and downs. We will walk in others' shoes and hear the words that have been spoken to them and by them and hopefully those words will touch us with the same magnitude. One word can make all the difference.

I have written the saying down that students have shared with me on scraps of paper, journals, my cell phone or tried to memorize them. Some of them have stopped me in my tracks when told to me, some are familiar but perhaps said in a different way. My hope is these words inspire those that read them and those that have shared them.

Words to Om by. Daily inspired words from everywhere.

Words to Om by. Daily inspired words from everywhere.

ACKNOWLEDGEMENTS

My high school English class teacher was the first person to read my writing and encourage me to pursue story telling. My father, who always sang, quoted poetry and is the best storyteller I have met. Mr. Rogers guided me every day after school to a land where everyone is treated equally and with kindness. Walt Disney inspired me to imagine other worlds where anything was possible. "Jonathan Livingston Seagull", who I listened to on record. Listening to that story taught me how to close my eyes and soar. Mozart whose music took me on visual stories of my creation all over the world. The lyrics of Dave Stewart and the passion of Annie Lennox taught me to be fearless and creative. The Four Agreements taught me the power of being impeccable with the word and the art of choosing words with precision. Every dictionary ever published, which I spent hours reading during my overnight shifts as a radio D.J. Amrit Desai and Swami Kripalu who taught me to speak with my soul. Shakespeare, who taught me love is fickle and the human condition timeless. The short life of my brother Todd taught me the gravity of each moment of these lives we lead. Diane Ross, for teaching me to meditate for the first time and encouraging me to self-publish. Mary Hays who believes that my gifts are worth sharing. Molly Knight, for inspiring me to pursue your passion and create your own lane in life. Caroline Michele taught me that generations apart in ages does not stop a true friendship and to seize the day, roll down the window and yell, "I Love Laguna Nigel!" I promised your words in print one day, your dream.

Words to Om by. Daily inspired words from everywhere.

Words to Om by. Daily inspired words from everywhere.

Troy Cox

- Amrit Yoga Master Teacher and Yoga Nidra Certified
- Creator of Sun Salute Yoga Studio
- Developed Safe Yoga School Teacher Training
- 500 Hour ERYT, Master Yoga teacher Amrit Institute.
- Certified by Yogi Amrit Desai and Kamini Desai in meditation Yoga Nidra
- Teaching Yoga since 2002
- Meditation studies with Diane Ross since 1995
- Published article contributor.
- Leader of yoga retreats internationally
- Author of 'The Y of Yoga; why yoga is popular.'

Words to Om by. Daily inspired words from everywhere.

BIOGRAPHY

Troy Cox, born in Virginia to military parents, spent his formative years in San Diego and Japan, experiences that shaped his diverse outlook on life. His poetic journey began in high school when a teacher recognized his talent, igniting a passion for writing that led to his first novel. Troy's dedication to yoga is profound, having completed over twelve teacher training programs and earning the prestigious title of 'Master Yogi' from the esteemed Yogi Amrit Desai, who bestowed upon him the yogic name 'Shanti,' meaning peace.

He aims to bring tranquility to a chaotic world, reflecting his belief in the transformative power of yoga. As an international yoga instructor, he has shared his expertise across the United States and beyond.

Master Teacher Troy Cox is the visionary behind the Total Engagement Concept™ system, a holistic approach that optimizes all aspects of being. This innovative system integrates the philosophical depths of yoga with personal training exercises, yogic postures, martial arts techniques, and Yoga Nidra therapy to unblock the mind. It also includes a meticulous focus on structural alignment and incorporates the Amrit Method of meditation in motion. Through this comprehensive approach, Troy guides his students to a fine-tuning of all their faculties, helping them achieve a harmonious balance in body, mind, and spirit.

Words to Om by. Daily inspired words from everywhere.

"The highest form of spiritual practice is self-observation, without judgement."

-Swami Kripalu

Words to Om by. Daily inspired words from everywhere.

FOREWARD

"In his latest book, Victorious – Words to Survive by, Troy Cox offers truly encouraging and insightful words. Here, he brings together many thoughts, ideas and quotes that seek to inspire, clarify, comfort and help to bridge the divide we often perceive between one another. Troy reminds us of and assures us of the threads that bind us together, the often unseen energy swirling in and through and around us. This meaningful connection can be acknowledged and even increased when we choose to walk with honesty and courage in our own lives and then seek to find the true commonalities we all share.

Troy is a rare find and someone I am honored to know. He strives to live all aspects of his life in integrity and with humility. In his classes, workshops, teachings and writings, Troy shares from a place of truth and vulnerability so we don't feel as alone in the struggle to more fully understand this extraordinary human journey. And, as he's written in these pages, the heart must remain open for us to connect at a meaningful level both with ourselves and with others. Yet, this requires both bravery and trust. Fortunately, Troy goes on to provide words and ways to help us keep our hearts open. And in doing so, we can find comfort in knowing that the very light of truth can bring us hope and guide us through the darkest of hours.

May this deeply caring and noble man's book, Victorious – Words to Survive by, give you the insights that you seek and the steadfast reminder that the open and loving heart will be rewarded with a peace, grace and well-being that can surpass even our own expectations.
Namaste…"

Mary Hayes
Intuitive Counselor/Medium/Author

Words to Om by. Daily inspired words from everywhere.

"I am honored to have been Troy's first meditation. He didn't know it at the time, but I had learned many of the same meditation techniques that he would also learn through his future yoga teacher, Amrit Desai, whom he met years later.

Troy may attribute his success to what he has learned through others, and that is partly true, but his main reason for being so successful is the realization of his authentic self. His journey through his own hells has strengthened him and made him more compassionate, but that's because he chose the path of love and not the path of bitterness. "

Diane L. Ross, author, *Meditations for Miracles*

"I've known Troy for 20 years and am so blessed to call him a friend. He's taught me yoga on the beaches of Carmel, California and in a thatched roof hut in Ubud, Bali.

So many spiritual teachers are different in class than they are in the outside world. Not Troy. He quite literally practices what he preaches: his life could be measured in deep breaths and sacred pauses. He's held me while I've cried through heartbreak, and celebrated with me as I realized some of my wildest dreams. He is a gentle soul with such a calming presence, and the wisdom he has to share is powerful.

It's been an honor to watch him grow as a teacher and fully embody everything it means to be a yogi."

Molly Knight, author, *The Dodgers-The Best Team Money can Buy. New York Best Seller.*

Words to Om by. Daily inspired words from everywhere.

Words to Om by. Daily inspired words from everywhere.

Two are better than one, because they have a good return for their toil. For if they fall, one will lift his fellow; but woe to him who is alone when he falls and has not another to lift him up. Again, if two lay together, they are warm; but how can one be warm alone? And though a man might prevail against one who is alone, two will withstand him. -- Ecclesiastes 4:9-12

Words to Om by. Daily inspired words from everywhere.

Words to Om by. Daily inspired words from everywhere.

CHAPTER ONE
PURIFICATION, WATER

"I am not what I think I am.
And I am not what you think I am.
I am what I think, you think, I am."

– Charles Horton Cooley

Words to Om by. Daily inspired words from everywhere.

A recent period of my life was so stressful and yet so educational at the same time. It all began when I found out that my landlord was being foreclosed on, and I would have to move. Moving out in ten days is not easy, and I could not have done it without the help of some friends and clients. Thank God for the help. I had begun the process of trying to buy my first home, a place I could stay. There comes a time in one's life when it is no longer fun to have instability, and I was ready to settle down for a few years in the same home in Southern Cali., a place I love. After months of looking and filling out paperwork, dealing with an unmotivated banker, and the uncertainty of whether I could qualify, I found out I had to wait until a future time to get more things in order before I could buy. I had chosen to live on friends' couches while this was going on, still working full time, with all my belongings scattered between a storage unit and two homes. Often, I found myself thinking, "I teach stress reduction, I can do this." Then I got sick.

It was what I thought was the worst flu I ever got. Traditionally, I heal myself, but this was only getting worse, so upon visiting a Dr., I found out I was one week away from having Pneumonia. Medication, teaching yoga, personal training, sleeping on couches…wow. Since I could not qualify at this time to buy my home, I needed to find a new place to rent. I have never been a fan of apartment complexes, so I needed to look for another privately owned condo. Meanwhile I considered the roommate idea, but after seeing several rooms for rent in other homes, I realized that at 20, a room for rent is a good idea, at 41, it is not going to work. At my wit's end, I got a call from a friend and client informing me that the unit next to hers was going for rent and she could talk to the owner for me.

Words to Om by. Daily inspired words from everywhere.

I had two weeks to move in, my friend is coming to visit from N.Y. for four days, I am working full-time and trying to get ready for my trip to Yoga school in Florida, and I have a falling out with a friend of mine, a disagreement. This is the friend that was going to help me move and drive me to the airport. Then it happened again: sickness. This one was worse than anything I ever experienced. I went from a little tickle in my throat to, four hours later, a full-blown sinus infection. Luckily, I was going to the Dr. the next day for a pain I had in my right heel since running my last Marathon in January. I left with an antibiotic prescription and a possible fractured foot.

I had one week to move myself in, find a new ride to the airport, try to repair my friendship, get foot extras, and am in pain from my sinuses to my toes, teach yoga, train people, and entertain a friend. My mantra becomes, 'breathe.... breathe.... breathe, let go'.

My visit with my friend from N.Y. was so much fun. I got all my belongings moved in before she got here (still in boxes, but in one place), and the fracture turned out to be treatable plantar fasciitis. Another friend drove me to the airport, and after antibiotics and an acupuncture treatment, the sinus infection went away, and with a cortisone shot in my foot, the pain had subsided. I made it through this rough spot using all that yoga has given me as tools to deal with stress.

It turns out I only lived in the new place for a year before the owner did the same thing as the last, Foreclosed, without notifying me until the bank started posting notices on the door despite me paying the landlady rent during the process and I had to move again. It turned out to be a string of moves and a minor setback in perspective to all the challenges life was about to bring me.

Reflecting, the only thing that kept me together, positive, and calm were the techniques I have learned since studying stress management. I often speak about these techniques to others in my attempts to be inspirational; I read about them and listen to my teacher's teachings, but rarely do I get to practice them as fully as I did in those months.

Words to Om by. Daily inspired words from everywhere.

Many times, I share my stress-dealing tips with others, but I never have to consciously practice them myself as they are ingrained in who I am, and I practice them without even having to try. They just happen. When stress confronts me, these tools are my response automatically after so many years of practicing and teaching them. This was put to the test recently when I had to deal with the dump truck full of situations within two months, any one of which could have stressed me out in my twenties, before I learned yoga, for months.

Looking back over those trying times, I can see they prepared me for the harder times that were ahead of me. The closing of my beloved yoga studio because of years-long construction by the city that prevented normal business function, moving across the country, losing my mother to cancer, and caring for my octogenarian father, who is slowly losing the ability to care for his most fundamental needs. We all can make a laundry list of stressors in life. It is easy to compare our stress to others in a one-upmanship of stress competition. That can add even more trauma to the pile. If they can be facilitated privately in a loving, safe, kind, and compassionate way, with tools that work for us, we can release them and then find the healing we need to recover and not relive them.

Trauma is a distraction like all external world stuff is. We can wallow in it, traumatize others with it, or find the healthiest way we can to release it and work on recovering, finding the person with the right tools for our unique trauma.

It comes down to having those who are equipped for our unique samskara (old, buried wound) to heal them with us. My skill set is not equipped to handle extreme, deep types of traumas. If you or someone you know is in serious need or mental health, please seek professional help. My hope is that this book becomes another tool in many readers tool bags that they can use regularly to navigate the stressful pitfalls of life.

Looking back on this story, I realize that I have gone through much worse situations. Within three years, I lost my mother, my father moved across the country to be near me, and he had to fight lung cancer. The three top stressors on the list. Whatever the stressor in our lives is, we need tools to deal with them. If we work hard, perhaps one day, we can achieve a non-reactive state and break the stress cycle.

How I get through the tough times:

1) Deal with situations head on: In my family, when we have conflict, we deal with it right then and there, even if it involves heated words, and passionate feelings, then we resolve it and move on. We work to let it go and not let it linger on and on. I realize; some people do not deal with conflict this way. Some run away from it and never resolve it. We have three choices: fight, flight, or deal. When we can deal with the situation at hand, talk it out, and find a solution, it can be released and resolved. I always remember the saying, it is not what happens to us, it is how we deal with it. Dealing with it is the only way to not carry it around, suppress it and have it manifest later. So, with each thing that came up for me, I tried to confront it, resolve it, and move on, not put it off until later, run away, or ignore it and hope it would go away on its own. Ruth Bader Ginsberg has taught generations how to get along with those who have opposite opinions in a powerful yet calm way. Never be afraid to stick to your morals and ethics and assert what you believe in, even if you are the only one doing so. But being able to do this in a calm and intelligent manner will ensure that you are heard and not adding to the noise.

2) Physically Shake it off: There is a ton of research to support this simple idea. We can release physical stress caused by situations in life through physical activity. Unresolved stress stuffed down and repressed can and will manifest as illness and emotional blockages that resurface later and result in repeating the same patterns of destructive behavior and required counseling. In Yoga, we call it Samskara. For me, it is my physical Yoga practice that releases stress in my body, joints, muscles, and mind. For others, it is running, boxing, dancing, swimming, or weightlifting. Whatever activity you can find, shake it off. Get it out of your mind for an hour, build up heat that burns out

Words to Om by. Daily inspired words from everywhere.

stress, get a massage, get it out of the physical body. The best I felt over these last two months was after teaching/ doing a very vigorous yoga class. In balance postures, our minds simply cannot think of anything else but being in the present moment, or we fall over.

3) Write it down: This is one I do not practice enough, but over the last two months, it has been a lifesaver. Put a notepad by the bed with a pen, make it the only thing on the nightstand. Every night, just before falling asleep, jot down a list of what you must do the next day, set it aside, do not analyze it, and then close your eyes and let it go. The next morning review your list but leave it on the nightstand. At the end of the day, cross off everything you accomplished, add whatever is unfinished on the list for the next day, then throw away the previous list and make a new one, close your eyes, and go to sleep. This way, you get out of your head, worrying about what you must do the next day, or about what you did not get done. It simply cannot sit there as you are trying to sleep and roll around in your mind. It is out of you and on a physical piece of paper. Simple, takes practice, but it works.

4) Date yourself: One day out of the week, have a date with yourself. I try on Sundays to take myself to the movies alone. I take myself to a simple place to eat, then go to a movie I want to see, have a bag of M&M's, and enjoy my own company. No scheduling with others, worrying about what they want to eat or what movie they want to see, just me and myself. This allows me to 'check out' for a couple of hours. I can reset my mind and relax. I tell myself thank you at the end. This is a practice I try to do at least twice a month and have made mandatory for years. I leave the phone in the car and simply 'check out'. It is like a reset button for my energy, allowing me to refocus on my wants and needs without the demands of external sources. Treat yourself the way you want to be treated, and then tell yourself thank you. In the end, all we have is ourselves anyway.

Words to Om by. Daily inspired words from everywhere.

5) Rest: The hardest one for me. Finding the right amount of time to rest the body, rest the mind, and rest the heart. Being a type A, I always want to go the extra mile and believe sleep is for when I am in the grave, but under times of stress, the body and mind need to sleep. Plain and simple, sleep heals all. The first thing the Dr. said to me was go home and sleep. Boy was he right.

6) Tool Bag: Fill up your tool bag with tools that work for you. Whenever I teach how to deal with stress I 'stress' the importance of finding tools that work for you. Humans have, for centuries, tried to find ways to deal with the stress of life in a productive and empowering way to avoid defeat.
From the ancient Greeks to the modern-day self-help aisle there are countless resources available to us with a little research and practice. Find the ones that work for you by practicing them. Here are the tools that work for me the most. Breathing consciously. It is more than just taking a deep breath and counting backward. Learn some techniques that involve a little bit of work. It distracts the brain from stress and preoccupies it with a task to complete. The stress is usually diminished if not gone by the end of the technique. My favorite is the straw breath. Check out my YouTube channel: Trainer Troy Yoga, for instructions. The other vital tool that I use all the time without even realizing I am doing it is mantra. Take some time and develop a word, poem, phrase, or prayer that brings you instant comfort and reminds you of what is truly important to you. Repeating these words, original words that you wrote or adopted yourself can interrupt the stress cycle powerfully, especially when spoken aloud. Author your own mantra, as your words will speak to you in the most powerful way. First, you can use or adopt someone else's words, such as the ones I include here. Experiment with them when stress comes your way. They do not have to be serious or spiritually inspired. They can simply be words that distract you from the stress monster in front of you. Humor works well, as does imagination, fantasy, love, sex, food, the beach, or anything that brings you joy, love, and comfort instead of stress. See if

Words to Om by. Daily inspired words from everywhere.

they worked for you to break the stress off at its start before it builds into a complete cycle.

In this chapter are some prayers, mantras, poems, and words that I and others use to inspire, uplift, and break up the stress cycle. I have written many of these and collected them from students in yoga class, mentors, and friends. I hope these simple techniques help you someday, so that your life is free of stress and that you can sleep.

Words to Om by. Daily inspired words from everywhere.

"Your' pain is the breaking of the shell that encloses your understanding." -Kahlil Gibran

"You can wash your hands. Don't be afraid to get them dirty."

-Lola Davis
(My Grandmother.)

Words to Om by. Daily inspired words from everywhere.

Raindrops by Troy Cox

Raindrops Gather in a huddle.
A slow slide towards gravity.
Diamond cut Moonlight.
Beams of opal radiating into the night.
Each individual drop culminating in the symphony of sound.
Dancing lit raindrops float in midair.
Elven Magic cast upon the land like shimmering diamonds.
Slow slide to gravity begins.
Individual drops descend.
Long streams of surrender.
Joy is in the air.
The individual drop melts into vastness.
Not lost, returning to what was once home.
Melt, merge and return.
The way we all go.

The Dew Drop by Caroline Michel

The leaf came tumbling down.
A drop of water fell shortly after.
The light beam illuminated the drop.
You are the light beam,
Upon the drop of water.

Words to Om by. Daily inspired words from everywhere.

"You are the result of what you say to yourself; not what others say about you."

Anonyms

"If you do the best you can, then angels can do no more."

- Virginia

This was my mother's favorite saying.

Words to Om by. Daily inspired words from everywhere.

'Accentuate the positive'

I think Bing Crosby said this and my mother used to always say it to me

-Brenda

'She unleashed her inner goddess and became the woman her soul knew she could be.'

Michelle Schaper

Words to Om by. Daily inspired words from everywhere.

'Enjoy each day by living up to your potential.'

-Charlotte

'Eat rice, be nice and let the good times roll.'

-Ed Cox
(My father.)

Words to Om by. Daily inspired words from everywhere.

'Yesterday's history, tomorrow is a mystery and today is a gift. We are glad to get the gift of today.'

-Mitzie

'I am enough! I am enough! I am enough!'

-Bonnie

Words to Om by. Daily inspired words from everywhere.

'Don't let your past define your future.'

-Kelly

'Are my thoughts, words, actions, and deeds serving my higher purpose? If not, can I change them?'

-Troy Cox

Words to Om by. Daily inspired words from everywhere.

Words to Om by. Daily inspired words from everywhere.

Can You Hear Me?

You feel a million miles away
Yet you're right next to me
I can feel your breath
Yet you don't speak
Where are you
I know your there
Yet you do not answer
Who is telling you to stay away
I plead, your silent
I beg, you whisper
I pour, you ignore
I throw a fit, you walk away
Why can't I reach you
My love has been silenced
No voice to tell my why
No words to explain
Cold emptiness
I feel but do not hear your words.
God, can you hear me?

-Troy Cox

Words to Om by. Daily inspired words from everywhere.

Swami Kripalu

This is an extraordinary story of how love and devotion can overcome a multitude of hardships and result in a life of inspiration. Swami Kripalu, lovingly called Bapuji was born into a large and devout Brahmin family in 1913. When he was seven years old he suffered the death of his father, Jamnaa's Majmundar which plunged Bapuji's family into dire financial circumstances.

When the pain of his family's poverty became too much for Bapuji to bear, he decided to drop out of school, give his life to God and find a way to make his family happy. Bapuji summed it up with these words,

"Although on rare occasions I might succumb to an urge and do something others disliked, I would immediately realize my mistake and apologize. Even after becoming a swami and the guru of thousands of disciplines, I still behave in a way that keeps others happy."
-Swami Kripalu

In childhood Bapuji loved chanting mantras and meditation. He often performed special pujas or ceremonies to the images of Krishna that were in his home. The devotion he inherited from his father and the musical influence of his older brother, who taught him the essentials of harmonium playing, turned his life in the direction of music, literature and yoga.

Words to Om by. Daily inspired words from everywhere.

"My father was a great devotee of the Lord. After becoming a swami and doing years of sadhana, or spiritual practice, I discovered that my father left me a great treasure—that of devotion or bhakti. The seed of bhakti that he planted within me has come into full bloom in my life…. Oddly enough, I have felt excruciating pain whenever I had to be sidetracked from my pursuit of music, literature, or yoga." -- Swami Kripalu

Bapuji taught himself to read and write by the age of ten years old and was daily reading a book of 200 or 300 pages. He excelled in his studies and learned what it took to be a good student… and until his death, considered himself a student of life, music, literature and yoga.

His legacy continues to live on in a living lineage and the hearts and minds of those who study his teachings.

"If you want to see your reflection in a mirror, you must keep the mirror steady. If you keep moving it back and forth, you'll miss your image. To properly study a subject, hold the mirror steady. That is, observe everything with a steady mind and dwell deeply on your subject."

Words to Om by. Daily inspired words from everywhere.

-Swami Kripalu

Hearing these stories about a legendary man that committed all he was to a spiritual quest resonated with me in a way that I felt was prompting me to act about something. It rang a bell that many wise folks, explorers and seekers had traveled the road of seeking answers before us, whose experience had been lost to the sands of time. What we could learn if those that quested for deeper meaning and experience had recorded their experience. This great teacher, Kripalu had written much about his experience, but only one book was translated into English. What are we missing out on because it is lost in translation?

That is the genesis of this book. What stories have others heard repeated that we do not know their source origin, or that we have heard over time that inspires others and keeps them going in tougher times? What do we reach that which uplifts us daily? What words of the past do we repeat without even realizing what their meaning is until we stop and investigate their meaning to us. This book is part inspiration, what comes to me during the last pose in yoga as a teacher, and part repetition, the phrases or sayings students have shared that they repeat, that uplift them and help them to feel better.

Words to Om by. Daily inspired words from everywhere.

Words to Om by. Daily inspired words from everywhere.

God is good.
All is well.
God is in control.

-Anonyms

Words to Om by. Daily inspired words from everywhere.

CHAPTER TWO
POSSIBILITIES, EARTH

Here is Where - Caroline Michel

Here is where we walked,
Here is where we ate,
Here is where we drank.
Here is where we laughed.
Here is where my heart is
Here is where my soul lives.

Words to Om by. Daily inspired words from everywhere.

The body is a machine, and there is a lot that we can do to help the machine run smoothly for longer. I try to think of the body as a unit of mechanical structure and function. The old song, "the leg bone is connected to the knee bone…" is fun but also helps us to see how all parts of the body are connected. The parts work in a fine orchestration to create movement of the structure. The body is organic, so it can move in unexpected ways and movements that it is not designed for or are not the safest for it to do. It is my job as the guide of our students to keep them safe in the strange shapes of yoga that I am asking them to move into and out of. I think less in anatomical terms and more in how the body is designed to function and move through space and time. If we are moving the body the way it is designed to move it will be safe.

    The body is alive and full of energy. It wants and is designed to move. Sitting still for an extended period is the least conducive for the health of the body. Everything about the design of the body says movement. Sitting still kills blood flow and neurologic connection. It causes bed sores and leads to depression. It is unhealthy to sit still for a long time. These poses are meant for movement. The yogis named them after nature, animals, earth, and wise people. All are meant to create the movement of energy. Each pose has its healing elements and needs to be activated by energetic expression.

I Love Being as Part of the Whole I Am that I Am

    Along with movement of the body it can be helpful to think or say a mantra or phrase that inspires and allows for energetic movement within, empowering and complimenting your physical movements.

Words to Om by. Daily inspired words from everywhere.

I am worth celebrating. I am worth everything. I am unique. In this whole world there is only one of me. There is no Being with my talents, experiences, and gifts. No one may take my place. God created only one of me. I have immense potential to love, care, create, grow, and sacrifice. I believe in my 'Self'. It does not matter my age, color of skin, my job, status, or whether this life parents loved me or not. Maybe they wanted to but couldn't. It doesn't matter what I have been, things I have done, mistakes made, people I have hurt. I am forgiven. I am accepted. I am okay. I am loved despite everything, or perhaps because of everything. I nourish my Being. I celebrate me. I begin now. I start anew every day. And I know what I say about myself is also true of every other being.

"In search of the divine we go everywhere. We go to the places of pilgrimage, sit in temples, follow many paths and disciplines- and ignore our bodies. Your body is the most sacred place of pilgrimage you'll ever come to. It is the dwelling place of the divine spirit; it is the temple of God. Go within and experience the glory of God within you."
-Yogi Amrit Desai

Words to Om by. Daily inspired words from everywhere.

Love Your Feet

The feet carry us everywhere, yet we hardly acknowledge their work. We don't think about them unless they complain. They are delicate little joints upon which rests all our body weight. The individual bones in the feet are as delicate as hummingbird wings, intricately designed for movement. The ankle through which passes all the tendons that control the foots movements is amazing in its structure and design. Robotics have the hardest time replicating their movements, and millions of dollars have been spent trying. Still the artificial intelligent creatures we try to create move clumsily as they try to match the superiority of human design.

So powerful are the feet that running is a sport, and speed is coveted. The fastest runners used to deliver messages across great divides before mechanical inventions. Dance is an art that demands so much of these joints called feet. But oh, how they make the dancer soar. As a human race, we have walked all over this planet, from the highest summits to the deepest caves. The feet are incredible. Yet we ignore them. Unless we step on a sharp object, twist an ankle, or stub a toe.

Take a moment and get to know your feet. Sit comfortably with naked feet. Focus on your feet for a moment. Feel all your toes, the long bones called phalanges. Let them wiggle. Watch them move. Amazing. Bring the bottom of the feet together in a butterfly shape with your knees bent to the side. Let the bottom of your feet touch. They rarely get to meet each other. Allow them to feel themselves touching, gripping your other foot.

Words to Om by. Daily inspired words from everywhere.

God is good.
All is well.
God is in control.

-Anonyms

Words to Om by. Daily inspired words from everywhere.

Spring by Caroline Michel

Spring is upon us
Let us not lust
Unless we love
Then we must
Oh well
We will not fuss

The Dove by Caroline Michel

I sent a dove of love
Over the yellow field of flowers.
The red tiled cluster of homes.
The dove paused for a moment
Over the home you call your own.
Then onward in is flight
Over the purple San Joaquin mountains.
The dove flew to the blue Pacific Ocean.

Words to Om by. Daily inspired words from everywhere.

As the Ravens Fly by Caroline Michel

As the raven's fly,
Free as they are.
No rules, no should haves, no should nots.
The only law the ravens need to obey,
Is to fly across the southern sky.
Before the sun has set,
They fly as if one being.
I wish I were as free
As the ravens.

Best Decision

"I have found that in any difficult situation, when I make the choice to do what is best for me, and honor my soul, that it ultimately is the best decision for everyone involved."

-Kristi Vanator

Words to Om by. Daily inspired words from everywhere.

"If you do the best you can, then angels can do no more."

-Virginia (My Mom's Saying)

"You are the holy essence of divine love."

- Diane Ross

My prayers when things are tough is to repeat over and over.

"Thy will be done"
-Alice Jean

Words to Om by. Daily inspired words from everywhere.

From The Secret Daily Teachings

To allow the Universe to move you in your life to happier and better things, you are going to need to look around you and appreciate the good things here and now. Seek the beautiful things and count the blessings of where you are. Dissatisfaction will not bring the happier and the better into your life. Dissatisfaction roots you to the spot where you currently are, but appreciation for what you have attracts the happier and better to you.
Remember that you are a magnet! Appreciation attracts appreciation!

Words to Om by. Daily inspired words from everywhere.

Grateful Dog's Eyes

Love is everywhere.
In a grateful dog's eyes.
In the last leaf that holds on to the tree in winter.
In a melody heard and remembered later in a quiet moment. - Jackie

Words to Om by. Daily inspired words from everywhere.

CHAPTER THREE
PROTECTION, FIRE

"In search of the divine we go everywhere. We go to the places of pilgrimage, sit in temples, follow many paths and disciplines-and ignore our bodies. Your body is the most sacred place of pilgrimage you'll ever come to. It is the dwelling place of the divine spirit; it is the temple of God. Go within and experience the glory of God within you."
-Yogi Amrit Desai

Words to Om by. Daily inspired words from everywhere.

Words to Om by. Daily inspired words from everywhere.

The Transformative Power of Movement

Transmutation is as sand is to Diamonds. There is a benefit to moving the body regularly; like the grains of sand, when we remain sedentary, we too begin to stiffen and become immobile. The human body is comprised of over three hundred joints allowing it to do what it was designed to do, move. So, many joints and so much movement available to us. Yet, our modern life dictates that we sit. Sit in an automobile, sit on the train, sit at work all day, and come home to sit in front of the television. With that much sitting we must schedule time to move the body. We buy expensive gym memberships, new workout clothes, new tennis shoes, and hire a trainer if we have any budget left. However we arrive at the physical practice, the lesson is the same. If you generate heat by moving, there is change. If left to sit, there is decomposition. The body is designed to move, so move it and things will change.

    Every new year at the gym is the mad rush of New Year's promises that never have a chance of coming true. We throw ourselves into a new routine. After the first thirty days, I often never see them again. It is so much easier to lay down on your mat and roll around however the body wants you to move. My practice has evolved into sitting on my mat and asking my body what it wants me to move. Sometimes, a whole beautiful flow comes out of my body that surprises me. Other times, it just tells me to be still and breathe.

> **"I practice yoga for my health. Maintaining flexibility, quieting my mind and breathing techniques."** - Michele H.

Words to Om by. Daily inspired words from everywhere.

"Is it helpful or hurtful?"

When I first started teaching kindergarten I had an amazing mentor and dear friend, Danielle Peeples. She was teacher of the year at Rosemont Elementary School in Orlando, a Title One school for underserved families. I was teaching at Orlando Day Nursery, a non-profit school for underserved downtown Orlando families, so we had similar students. Whenever she encountered a behavior issue with a child she would ask them if they were being helpful or hurtful. She guided children to solve a myriad of problems themselves. Children want to be helpful. I've found that it works for every adult situation as well. Tragically we lost Danielle to cancer in 2015. Her philosophy, "Is it helpful or hurtful?" lives on. Let's all be helpful.
 Eileen Marie Simoneau

Words to Om by. Daily inspired words from everywhere.

My personal mantra has been the last few years:

" Aspire to inspire before you expire. "

-Alice Jean

Worry is like a rocking chair. You expend a lot of energy on it but travel nowhere. - -

-Anonyms

If you don't like the track playing in your mind, change it.

-Diane Ross

Words to Om by. Daily inspired words from everywhere.

I love the following quote from Sylvia, it reminded me of the beautiful Chaste trees that Master Gardener Sandy gave me. One side of the leaf is a cool green and the underside is a lavender color. If you do not like one side, remember there is always another side. Just like the idea of transmutation, turning one thing into another. Silica into diamonds. It is possible to use the negative to remind us of the positive in life or turn the negative energy into a victorious energy.

Websters defines this process as:
Transmutation noun
:an act or instance of **transmuting** or being **transmuted**: such as
a: the conversion of base metals into gold or silver
b: the conversion of one element or nuclide into another either naturally or artificially- Merriam Websters Dictionary

"Every leaf has another side"
-Sylvia Klein Olkin

'Sylvia was my pre-natal yoga teacher. I loved what she did so much that I became a doula and teacher myself. She was big into visualization in birth and life, so it more of a visualization than a 'saying' but I say it to myself all time.' -Linda Horn

Words to Om by. Daily inspired words from everywhere.

Shiva Temples by Troy Cox

Left Pondicherry
Dancing Shiva Temple Dharasuram Sri Airavatesvara Temple
Dancing Shiva Air temple of Nataraja
The fearsome warrior prince
who overthrew his father, the God, in a fearsome rage?
AD 907- 1310 constructed
A beautiful puja happening with drumming.
Westerners are being initiated to chanting.
Fires, lights, incense, beauty abounds.
Walking with Gurudev.
Doing Yoga at the Gas Station
Jai Shiva!

From Julie Nussbaum Hanson:

> **"Out of suffering have emerged the strongest souls: the most massive characters are scarred with scars."**
>
> - Kahlil Gibran

Words to Om by. Daily inspired words from everywhere.

"It is always darkest before the dawn."

-Contributed by Mary Hayes

Words to Om by. Daily inspired words from everywhere.

Words to Om by. Daily inspired words from everywhere.

The Hardest Meditation I know:

Transmuting Fire into Love: A Self-Affirmation Practice

Meditation Prompt:
Observe any negative self-beliefs and self-talk arise, imagine them as a fire. Instead of letting this fire consume you, use it as fuel to transform your thoughts into love for yourself. Say this meditation until it becomes believable:

"I, [insert your name], love you, just as you are. Nothing needs to change, and I mean it."

Reflect on this: Recognize that these negative beliefs are opportunities to practice self-love.

Journal Exercise:
Write your affirmation here with your name:

(Read it aloud a few times, then silently repeat it until you feel the cool calming effect of love replacing the fire of negativity.)

Words to Om by. Daily inspired words from everywhere.

Your Victorious Words: A Reflection
Now, it's your turn to reflect:

1. Pause and Reflect: Take a moment to consider the words or phrases that have fueled your victories in challenging times. These might be personal mantras, family mottos, or words that have empowered you to rise above adversity.

2. Write Them Down: Capture these words on paper. Let them flow freely without judgment and recognize the triumph each one represents.

3. Embrace Their Power: Reflect on the victories these words have helped you achieve. Think about how they've guided you through trials and celebrate the strength they continue to give you.

These words are more than just phrases—they're declarations of your resilience and victory.

Words to Om by. Daily inspired words from everywhere.

YOUR VICTORIOUS WORDS
A REFLECTION JOURNAL

Who or what inspires these words?

When did you first hear these words?

How do these words make you feel victorious?

Words to Om by. Daily inspired words from everywhere.

Words to Om by. Daily inspired words from everywhere.

CONTACT

Troy Cox

www.trainertroy.com

troycoxyoga@gmail.com

*Please email me your yoga stories, questions, comments and feedback. Subscribe to my YouTube channel 'TRAINERTROYYOGA' for instructional videos and meditations. I am available to book for speaking and teaching engagements. May you be blessed.

Safe Yoga School

www.safeyogaschool.com

safeyogaschool@gmail.com

Find out about hosting a Safe Yoga Teacher Training at your local studio or in person in a private training. My Safe Yoga Teacher Training Program has generated income flow for new studios, helping them thrive and serve more.

Words to Om by. Daily inspired words from everywhere.

Made in the USA
Columbia, SC
11 March 2025